SUPREME COURT CASES

THROUGH PRIMARY SOURCES™

Brown  Board of Education

The Case Against School Segregation

Wayne Anderson

rosen central
Primary Source™
The Rosen Publishing Group, Inc., New York

In loving memory of my dearly departed mother, Brenda Anderson, and for my father, Joshua George Anderson, and the three enduring mother figures in my life: Jean Grant, Jasmine Anderson, and Jennifer Anderson

Published in 2004 by The Rosen Publishing Group, Inc.
29 East 21st Street, New York, NY 10010

Copyright © 2004 by The Rosen Publishing Group, Inc.

First Edition

All rights reserved. No part of this book may be reproduced in any form without permission in writing from the publisher, except by a reviewer.

Unless otherwise attributed, all quotes in this book are excerpted from court transcripts.

Library of Congress Cataloging-in-Publication Data

Anderson, Wayne, 1966–
Brown v. Board of Education: the case against school segregation / by Wayne Anderson.— 1st ed.
   p. cm. — (Supreme Court cases through primary sources)
Includes bibliographical references and index.
ISBN: 978-1-4358-3646-4
1. Brown, Oliver, 1918– —Trials, litigation, etc. 2. Topeka (Kans.) Board of Education—Trials, litigation, etc. 3. Discrimination in education—Law and legislation—United States. I. Title: Brown versus Board of Education. II. Title. III. Series.
KF228.B76A736 2003
344.73'0798—dc21

2003000219

Manufactured in the United States of America

Contents

Introduction 4

① Jim Crow 8

② The NAACP Challenges Segregation 14

③ The NAACP's Case Against Segregation 24

④ The Case for the States 32

⑤ Rearguments and a Decision 40

⑥ Implementation and Impact 49

Glossary 55

For More Information 57

For Further Reading 58

Bibliography 59

Primary Source Image List 60

Index 62

Introduction

Throughout the history of the United States, African Americans have struggled for basic civil rights. Between 1619 and 1865, African Americans sought freedom from slavery by running away from the plantations where they were held, engaging in rebellions, joining forces with abolitionists to create escape routes and safe houses for other slaves, and eventually fighting as soldiers in the Civil War. Since the end of the Civil War, when slavery was officially made illegal, African Americans have fought against discrimination in a constant effort to secure equality under American law. These efforts range from individual acts of defiance to street riots to organized acts of protests, such as demonstrations and civil disobedience.

Often, the African American struggle for equality is played out in the Supreme Court. The job of the Court is to

Introduction

interpret the U.S. Constitution, the supreme law of the land. Black citizens have often turned to the Supreme Court for protection from state and federal laws that they felt violated their constitutional rights. In doing so, they have often pointed to three constitutional amendments that are known collectively as the Civil War Amendments. The Civil War Amendments are the Thirteenth, Fourteenth, and Fifteenth Amendments. They were approved soon after the Civil War to raise African Americans to an equal stature with whites in the eyes of the law. These amendments abolished slavery (Thirteenth), forbade the states from denying anyone "equal protection under the laws" (Fourteenth), and gave African Americans the right to vote (Fifteenth). However, the Supreme Court has not always been sympathetic to African American claims of inequality, and some of its decisions have had a devastating impact on the daily lives of African Americans.

One such decision came in the 1896 case of *Plessy v. Ferguson*, in which the Supreme Court ruled that states could enforce the segregation of blacks and whites on intrastate railroads as long as the accommodations were roughly equal for each group. As had been the widespread practice even before the decision, the states, and eventually the courts, emphasized the "separate" part of the law more than the requirement of "equal." The Supreme Court's decision undermined the Fourteenth Amendment and allowed states to legally treat blacks as second-class citizens. The decision extended to many other parts of life, and African Americans faced limits in their access to everything from jobs, housing, and education to such basic amenities as parks, theaters, and even water fountains.

Brown v. Board of Education

In this cartoon, a white businessman pushes an African American man into the street, preventing him from going near white establishments posting signs declaring that housing, school, public accommodations, and job opportunities are all restricted. Created by Herbert Block and published in the Washington Post on September 6, 1963, the cartoon captures the far-reaching impact that the Supreme Court's decision in Plessy v. Ferguson in 1896 had on African American life.

Introduction

However, the Supreme Court reversed itself in 1954 when it outlawed segregation in public education in the case of *Brown v. Board of Education of Topeka, Kansas*. Considered one of the most important decisions of the Supreme Court, the ruling gave a boost to the civil rights movement in the United States. It is widely seen not only as a victory for the African American struggle for civil rights but also as a major step forward in achieving the American ideal of equality.

Jim Crow

1

Many segregation laws, called Jim Crow laws, were already in place throughout the South before the Supreme Court's decision in *Plessy v. Ferguson*. In fact, segregation emerged immediately after the Civil War. The South, which had seceded (withdrawn) from the United States before the war, attempted to impose segregation by adopting laws known as black codes. The black codes limited the physical and economic freedom of the freedmen, or former slaves. Under Reconstruction, a program for reunifying the country after the war, Congress struck down the codes and extended civil rights to blacks. But Reconstruction lasted only about twelve years (1865–1877), and with its end came the return of the laws now known as Jim Crow laws. By 1896, when the *Plessy* case was heard, all the southern states had passed laws that required segregation on at least some of their railroads.

Jim Crow

This is a photograph of the Rex Theatre in Leland, Mississippi. During segregation, establishments across the United States, though mostly in the South, bore signs that announced what race they catered to. Although it is possible that the theater was owned by an African American, it is more likely that its owner was white. The photograph was taken in November 1939 by Marion Post Wolcott.

JIM CROW'S REACH

Plessy v. Ferguson gave constitutional approval to the segregation of intrastate trains, and the southern states wasted no time in extending segregation to other areas of public life. Soon, there were laws that limited where blacks could live, work, play, eat, shop, and even sit down to rest tired legs. Blacks were not allowed to enter hotels, theaters, schools, and restaurants reserved for whites. They could not seek treatment in white hospitals, could not be buried in white cemeteries, and could not use certain parks or swimming pools. Blacks and whites worshiped in separate

Brown v. Board of Education

This 1936 photograph shows a flag outside the window of the NAACP's New York headquarters announcing the lynching of an African American. There are nearly four thousand recorded cases of lynching during the Jim Crow era, although it is widely believed that many thousands of others were similarly killed.

churches. Even in places used by both races, such as train stations, blacks were forced to use separate entries, waiting rooms, and rest rooms before riding in separate cars on the trains.

In every instance, the facilities assigned to blacks were inferior to those that were set aside for whites. Moreover, the southern states instituted obstacles to prevent blacks from exercising other constitutional rights, such as voting, or serving on juries.

The motivating force behind Jim Crow laws was white supremacy. Jim Crow laws were rigidly enforced to keep blacks in positions of inferiority. African Americans who broke or tried to break the laws faced the possibility of arrest, lynching, and public punishment at the hands of a mob. Many of the arrests and most of the lynching ended in the death of the offender. According to Waldo E. Martin Jr. in *Brown v. Board of Education: A Brief History with Documents*, "Jim Crow also meant the suppression of successful as well as assertive blacks as 'uppity' and 'getting out of their place.'" Many were lynched on trumped-up charges or were burned out of their homes and businesses by white mobs.

Perhaps the arena in which segregation was most visible, and most damaging, was public education. The attitude of most policy makers in the South (and many in the North) was that education was wasted on African Americans, whom they regarded as not being much more than a source for cheap labor. Accordingly, the southern states spent comparatively little on public schools for blacks.

Black schools were inferior in every way. Typically, they were housed in rundown buildings that lacked adequate heating and plumbing. The teachers were underpaid and often faced overcrowded classrooms and a shortage of teaching aids. The schools offered fewer subjects than the all-white schools, and black students were always behind white students in terms of the level of instruction. Commenting on the state of education for African Americans at the beginning of the twentieth century, civil rights leader W. E. B. Du Bois notes in his book *The Souls of Black Folk*:

> The Negro colleges, hurriedly founded, were inadequately equipped, illogically distributed, and of varying efficiency and grade; the normal and high schools were doing little more than common-school work, and the common schools were training but a third of the children who ought to be in them, and training these often too poorly.

Brown v. Board of Education

This photograph shows a one-room school for blacks in rural Georgia around 1941. The school's only teacher instructs children of various ages in this ramshackle building. Notice that the students do not have desks.

Du Bois also noted that for every dollar that was spent per black child, $4 was spent per white child.

SURVIVING AND RESISTING JIM CROW

Jim Crow was not an easy or acceptable condition for black Americans to tolerate. But the need to survive often meant finding ways to avoid the violence and terror that lurked around them. In most instances, southern blacks tried to avoid engaging whites as much as possible. This approach made it necessary for blacks to develop their own institutions, such as schools,

Jim Crow

businesses, and community organizations, to meet their most pressing needs. Soon, many black communities had their own centers of commerce that typically included barbers, hairdressers, insurance companies, banks, social clubs, grocery stores, funeral parlors, and volunteer fire departments. Black newspapers sprang up to cover stories from an African American perspective and to make public service announcements.

In the presence of whites, many blacks assumed a sort of nervous, submissive posture, holding their heads down, avoiding eye contact, and addressing even a young white child as "sir" or "ma'am." Jim Crow required African Americans to wait in stores until all the white customers were served. Even then, they wouldn't ask for help until being first addressed by the store clerk. Survival also meant enduring being called "boy," "girl," and often "nigger" without showing offense.

However, the need to survive did not stifle resistance to Jim Crow or break down the determination of African Americans to win back the civil rights that had been lost after 1876. Much of the resistance took the form of individual acts of defiance at the risk of arrest, lynching, or loss of employment. Often, the fight was on a local level and took place in district courts, city halls, and county boardrooms. Black churches and newspapers were used to spread the word on the street to other communities in the South and ultimately to the North. Over time the challenges to segregation grew more organized, eventually reaching a national scale by 1909, when the National Association for the Advancement of Colored People (NAACP) was born.

The NAACP Challenges Segregation

2

Originally called the National Negro Committee, the NAACP was founded in 1909 by a group of white liberals and prominent blacks, including W. E. B. Du Bois. It was created in part as a response to a series of anti-black race riots, with the intent of securing the rights guaranteed in the Thirteenth, Fourteenth, and Fifteenth Amendments for all people. After establishing its national office in New York City, the NAACP quickly went to work attacking segregation on several fronts. These included bringing lawsuits that challenged discriminatory practices, lobbying Congress and the president for favorable actions, and setting up satellite branches throughout the country to remain up-to-date with local issues. The NAACP also launched a number of publicity campaigns through the media, primarily in its own journal, *The Crisis*, which was first edited by Du Bois.

The NAACP Challenges Segregation

The NAACP's early efforts, including its involvement in a number of court victories, soon established it as the leading African American civil rights organization and an important legal advocate. The organization grew rapidly, and by 1919, it had approximately 90,000 members in more than 300 branches. Throughout the 1920s, the NAACP conducted many civil rights lawsuits at the local level and aggressively, though unsuccessfully, lobbied Congress to pass an anti-lynching law.

An NAACP member, wearing a sandwich board sign, gives an African American man a pamphlet and encourages him to join the organization. During its first decade of existence, the NAACP carried out an aggressive and successful membership drive that included this sort of on-the-street recruitment.

A FOCUS ON EDUCATION

In 1930, under the guidance of its two leading lawyers, Charles Houston and Thurgood Marshall, the NAACP decided to challenge segregation in public schools. First on the agenda was to get state and local governments to provide facilities for African American children that were equal to those provided for white children. Similarly, the organization sought to win equal pay for African American teachers.

Brown v. Board of Education

This is the cover of the first issue of *The Crisis, the monthly magazine of the NAACP, which was published in November 1910. The magazine was edited by W. E. B. Du Bois, who wrote in its pages that "the object of this publication is to set forth those facts and arguments which show the danger of race prejudice, particularly as manifested today toward colored people."*

The NAACP Challenges Segregation

Given the obvious differences in the quality of schooling, these were easy cases for the NAACP. However, they were significant because they built court records that documented that, across the South, states were shortchanging blacks in violation of the "separate but equal" principle established by the *Plessy v. Ferguson* decision of 1896.

Following this strategy of equalization, the NAACP won several important court victories involving graduate schools. According to Kate Tuttle in an online article entitled "Brown v. Board of Education" on www.Africana.com, "By demanding equal facilities on the graduate level, Houston hoped to force states into a difficult decision: either build expensive new black professional schools or allow qualified African Americans to enroll in previously all-white law, medical, and other graduate schools." In most instances, the eventual result was that the graduate schools were ordered to open their doors to African Americans. Even in the few instances in which a state was willing to build a separate graduate school for blacks, the NAACP's lawyers successfully convinced the

As the NAACP's chief counsel, Thurgood Marshall led the legal charge against segregation that brought about the landmark Supreme Court decision in Brown v. Board of Education in 1954. Marshall became the first African American Supreme Court justice in 1967.

Brown v. Board of Education

What Are Our Immediate Goals?

1. To mobilize five million Negroes into one militant mass for pressure.
2. To assemble in Chicago the last week in May, 1943, for the celebration of

"WE ARE AMERICANS – TOO" WEEK

And to ponder the question of Non-Violent Civil Disobedience and Non-Cooperation, and a Mass March On Washington.

WHY SHOULD WE MARCH?

15,000 Negroes Assembled at St. Louis, Missouri
20,000 Negroes Assembled at Chicago, Illinois
23,500 Negroes Assembled at New York City
Millions of Negro Americans all Over This Great Land Claim the Right to be Free!

FREE FROM WANT!
FREE FROM FEAR!
FREE FROM JIM CROW!

"Winning Democracy for the Negro is Winning the War for Democracy!" — A. Philip Randolph

The NAACP's success at challenging segregation in courts helped to foster a climate for mass mobilization against Jim Crow. This 1941 flier called on African Americans to participate in a protest in Washington, D.C., against discrimination in hiring in the defense industry, the U.S. military, and the government. The march was called off after President Franklin D. Roosevelt issued an executive order that banned such discrimination.

courts that these institutions could not be equal to the white establishments.

FOUR PIVOTAL CASES

With these victories in hand, the NAACP decided to make a more direct challenge to segregation. In 1939, the organization created a legal defense fund, headed by Thurgood Marshall, specifically to fight segregation laws. By 1948, the NAACP was no longer satisfied with forcing states to provide equal accommodations for blacks. It was time to seek a reversal of the *Plessy*

The NAACP Challenges Segregation

v. Ferguson decision. To accomplish this, the NAACP chose to spearhead four class-action lawsuits involving segregated elementary schools. They were *Briggs v. Elliott*; *Brown v. Board of Education of Topeka, Kansas*; *Belton v. Gebhart* and *Bulah v. Gebhart* (which were tried together and known as the Delaware cases); and *Davis v. County School Board of Prince Edward County, Virginia*. These four cases would eventually reach the Supreme Court under the name *Brown v. Board of Education of Topeka, Kansas*.

Briggs v. Elliott

Briggs v. Elliott was the first of the cases to go to trial. It came from Clarendon County, South Carolina, where blacks accounted for 70 percent of the population. Clarendon County's school board chairman, R. W. Elliott, was sued for failing to provide a school bus for African American children. Thurgood Marshall had heard the story and became interested in the conditions of black schools in Clarendon County.

What he found out was appalling. More than one-third of the black population was illiterate. The school board spent $179 per year to educate each white child and only $43 per black child. Moreover, black students had to pay fees to use textbooks while white students had free access to them. The board provided more than thirty school buses for white students and none for blacks. The average class size was twenty-eight students at the white schools and forty-seven students at the black schools, yet white teachers earned two-thirds more than black teachers. White schools were housed in modern buildings while the black schools were held in dilapidated shacks that lacked in-door plumbing.

Brown v. Board of Education

Marshall convinced twenty citizens to sign a petition to file a lawsuit against Elliott. The case was tried in the U.S. district court in Charleston, South Carolina, before a three-judge panel. Marshall decided to try the case himself. In court, he called witnesses to testify about the inferior conditions of Clarendon County's black schools and about how those conditions had damaging psychological effects on black children. He argued, "The Negro child is made to go to an inferior school; he is branded in his own mind as inferior [and] this sets up a roadblock in his mind which prevents his ever feeling he is equal."

The school board admitted that the black schools were inferior and that the state was considering legislation to improve the schools. However, its lawyer called witnesses who testified that placing white children and black children together in the same school would lead to social unrest.

The judges decided by a vote of two to one in favor of the school board. Thurgood Marshall appealed this decision to the Supreme Court

Brown v. Board of Education of Topeka

In 1950, Oliver Brown tried to register his seven-year-old daughter, Linda, in an all-white school that was seven blocks from his home in Topeka, Kansas. The school refused to admit Linda because she was African American. She was forced to return to the all-black school that she had attended the previous two years. That school was a mile away from Linda's home. To get there, she had to walk six blocks, crossing a number of busy railroad tracks, to get to the nearest bus stop for a half-hour ride.

The NAACP Challenges Segregation

Upset that his daughter was denied entry into the all-white school, Oliver Brown joined a group of African American parents who sued the Topeka Board of Education. They were represented in court by two of Thurgood Marshall's assistants, Robert Carter and Jack Greenberg. Schoolchildren and other witnesses testified about how difficult and dangerous it was to get to the black schools. The NAACP lawyers tried to show that segregation fostered a feeling of inferiority in black children.

In response, the Topeka Board of Education argued that the conditions and facilities of its African American schools were roughly equal to those of its white schools. Although the court admitted that the segregated schools "had a detrimental effect upon the colored children," it ruled against the NAACP, arguing that the near equality of the black and white schools made their segregation constitutional.

This 1954 photograph shows ten-year-old Linda Brown and her six-year-old sister, Terry Lynn, walking along railroad tracks in Topeka, Kansas, to get to the nearest point where they could catch the bus to the Monroe School.

The Delaware Cases

The Delaware cases refer to two lawsuits, *Belton v. Gebhart* and *Bulah v. Gebhart*, that were tried together in the U.S. district

Brown v. Board of Education

court in Wilmington, Delaware, on October 22, 1951. The trial involved eleven plaintiffs from two Delaware towns who accused their board of education of providing inferior education for their children. Their charges were similar to those of the plaintiffs in the *Briggs* case, and their witnesses testified about the inadequate conditions of the schools. Again, NAACP lawyers Jack Greenberg and Louis Redding presented an expert witness who testified about the injury that segregated schools inflicted on black children. In these cases, however, the ruling went in favor of the NAACP's clients. The school board was ordered to admit the children of the eleven plaintiffs into the community's white public schools. The presiding judge, Collins Seitz, said, "I believe the 'separate but equal' doctrine in education should be rejected, but I believe its rejection must come from that [Supreme] Court." It was a good win for the NAACP. Delaware appealed the decision.

Davis v. County School Board of Prince Edward County

The *Davis* case was born out of a two-week strike by all 450 students of the Robert R. Moton High School in Prince Edward County, Virginia. Filed and handled by the NAACP's Spottswood Robinson on behalf of 117 of those students, the lawsuit demanded the immediate desegregation of Prince Edward County's schools. The NAACP adopted the same strategy in this trial as it had used in the other three.

The defense lawyers presented witnesses who testified about the county's commitment to the education of African Americans before attacking the lawsuit as NAACP propaganda.

The NAACP Challenges Segregation

The court ruled in favor of the school board, arguing that segregation in Virginia was part of the state tradition, was not prejudicial to blacks, and did not cause harm to either race. The NAACP also appealed this case to the Supreme Court.

THE SUPREME COURT AGREES TO HEAR THE CASES

On June 9, 1952, the Supreme Court agreed to hear the appeals of the lower court decisions in *Briggs v. Elliott* and *Brown v. Board of Education*, scheduling them for oral arguments in early October. Days before the scheduled hearing, the Court also accepted the *Davis* case and postponed the hearing to December. In November, the Court added the Delaware cases to its schedule and decided to hear all four cases together as *Brown v. Board of Education of Topeka, Kansas*. According to James Tackach in his book *Brown v. Board of Education*, "The Court used the Topeka case in the title so that the trial would not appear to concern an issue limited to the South." With this case, the Court would make a decision that would affect the entire country.

The NAACP's Case Against Segregation

3

Although only four NAACP lawyers—Thurgood Marshall, Robert Carter, Spottswood Robinson, and Jack Greenberg—would make oral presentations to the Court, the NAACP used a team of more than twenty lawyers to prepare the briefs, or written legal arguments, for the case. For four months, the group of lawyers spent long days researching previous Supreme Court and lower court decisions that they could use as precedents in their quest to overturn the *Plessy v. Ferguson* decision. Their goal was to bring an end to segregation in the United States, at least in public education. Many of the lawyers were driven by the thought that losing such an important case could deal a severe blow to civil rights, but everyone agreed that the case was winnable.

The NAACP's Case Against Segregation

Colonel Benjamin Davis Jr. (left) and Captain Edward Gleed of the all-black 332nd Fighter Pilot Squadron, known as the Tuskegee Airmen, pose by a fighter plane at their air base in southern Italy in 1945 during World War II. The heroics of black servicemen, including and especially the Tuskegee Airmen, during the war gave boost to the antisegregation movement among African Americans and within the country at large.

ADVANTAGES FOR THE NAACP

Thurgood Marshall and his band of lawyers had good reasons to be optimistic. Notwithstanding the prevailing attitudes toward blacks in the South, recent social and political trends across the country suggested that the environment was ripe for change.

The participation of African Americans in World War II in the early 1940s shed new light on the roles of blacks in American society. Before the war was over, the ground troops

Brown v. Board of Education

were integrated. Black and white American soldiers were fighting side by side on the battlefields.

Also, African Americans used the democratic ideals held by the United States to fight racism at home. In taking strong stances against Nazism, Communism, Fascism, and international racism, the United States's political leaders were forced to confront the contradiction between what it preached to the rest of the world and the reality of racism within the country. This hypocrisy was further driven home in an influential 1944 book called *An American Dilemma* by Gunnar Myrdal. In addition, more and more social scientists and other intellectuals began rejecting the works of earlier social scientists, who had argued that blacks were by nature inferior to whites. Racism was losing its appeal.

Perhaps the most encouraging sign for the NAACP was the Supreme Court itself. The high court had become more liberal since its ruling in *Plessy v. Ferguson*. (The Supreme Court is considered to be liberal when a majority of the justices regard the Constitution as a flexible framework that can adapt to changing times and social conditions.)

In addition, a series of rulings in favor of the NAACP seemed to signal the Supreme Court's growing intolerance for segregation. Two of these decisions, *Sweatt v. Painter* and *McLaurin v. Oklahoma State Regents for Higher Education*, both announced in 1950, could serve as precedents to undermine *Plessy*'s "separate but equal" doctrine. In both cases, which involved graduate schools, the Court ruled that equality was determined not only by the physical features and the curriculum (collection of courses) of the schools

The NAACP's Case Against Segregation

This 1948 photograph shows G. W. McLaurin, an African American, seated in an anteroom away from his white classmates at the University of Oklahoma. In 1950, the Supreme Court ruled that Oklahoma had violated McLaurin's constitutional rights by mandating that kind of segregation by law.

but also by other factors such as the reputation of the faculty and the influence of the alumni.

THE NAACP'S ARGUMENTS

Despite their optimism, the lawyers for the NAACP knew that victory was not a sure thing. *Plessy v. Ferguson* was still the law of the land, and the southern states had shown that they would go to extraordinary lengths to keep it that way. Although the Court had shown great sympathy for the NAACP's position, it seemed reluctant to go the distance in overturning *Plessy* outright.

Brown v. Board of Education

Making such a move could result in significant upheaval to the country's educational system and could even lead to widespread unrest in a resistant South. Moreover, although the Court could order the integration of schools, it had no direct power to enforce implementation.

The NAACP supplied four briefs, one for each of the cases involved in *Brown v. Board of Education of Topeka, Kansas*. In oral arguments, Carter spoke for the case from Kansas, Marshall for the South Carolina case, Robinson for the Virginia case, and Greenberg for the Delaware cases. The NAACP's constitutional claims were based on Section 1 of the Fourteenth Amendment, which reads:

> All persons born or naturalized in the United States, and subject to the jurisdiction thereof, are citizens of the United States and of the State wherein they reside. No State shall make or enforce any law which shall abridge the privileges or immunities of citizens of the United States; nor shall any State deprive any person in life, liberty, or property, without due process of law, nor deny to any person within its jurisdiction the equal protection of the laws.

In effect, the amendment granted citizenship to African Americans and required the state laws to treat them as equals to whites and all other citizens.

In all four cases, the NAACP argued that racial segregation in public schools reduces the benefits of public education to African Americans solely on the basis of race, violating the Fourteenth Amendment. They further argued that the great

The NAACP's Case Against Segregation

These two photographs of elementary schools in South Boston, Virginia, taken sometime between 1920 and 1940, show the differences in the accommodations for black and white students during segregation. The white school (top) is a modern, multistoried, well-built concrete structure. The black school (bottom) is an outdated wood structure on stilts that appears to be somewhat tilted. It is likely that the building was poorly heated and lacked modern plumbing.

Brown v. Board of Education

differences in the funding and physical conditions between black schools and white schools clearly demonstrated that black children were denied equal educational opportunities. Consequently, the segregation subjected black students to psychological damage by imposing on them feelings of inferiority and personal humiliation. This very consequence was another example of states denying equal protection under the law—that is, only black children were being psychologically injured by the state.

In the brief for Kansas's case, the NAACP argued that the Supreme Court's decisions in *Sweatt* and *McLaurin* had replaced *Plessy* as the relevant precedents. According to this argument, it did not matter that the separate facilities for blacks and whites were virtually equal. As the Court had established in those cases, equality was defined as much by intangible factors such as reputation and the psychological damage of discrimination as it was by funding, structure, and curriculum. Therefore, since the district court had agreed that segregation harmed black students and placed them at a disadvantage, it was in error not to have ruled segregation in Topeka as illegal.

In addition, the NAACP lawyers suggested that it would seem illogical for the Court to have ruled (in *Sweatt* and *McLaurin*) that a segregated school denied black graduate students their basic human rights yet let the separate but equal principle stand with regard to elementary and high school students.

The NAACP lawyers, especially Marshall, are said to have performed well in their appearances before the justices. Of Marshall's performance, Richard Kluger notes in *Simple Justice*: "On this day, he was at his best. He took the offensive

The NAACP's Case Against Segregation

from the start and he held it throughout the argument." The long days of preparation seemed to have paid off.

AN ASSIST FROM THE FEDERAL GOVERNMENT

The federal government filed an amicus curiae brief largely in support of the NAACP's position. (An amicus curiae, which is Latin for "friend of the court," is someone or an entity that is not a party to a lawsuit but who submits a point of view for the court to consider.) Written by one of President Harry Truman's assistant solicitor generals, the brief made three main points:

- The Court did not have to face the question of overruling *Plessy v. Ferguson*. It could remedy the inequalities found in South Carolina, Delaware, and Virginia by ordering the superior white schools to admit the black children involved in the cases until the states raised the black schools to a level equal to the white schools.
- If the Court wanted to tackle *Plessy* in this case, then it should "rid the nation of the noxious precedent" because separate but equal could not be fairly achieved.
- If the Court chose to reverse *Plessy*, it did not have to order an immediate end to segregation. The dismantling of Jim Crow should be done over a reasonable period of time to allow for an orderly transition.

Clearly, the federal government's stand could only be beneficial to the NAACP's case. Its introduction into the case made it clear that the government would be willing to help enforce an integration order from the Court.

The Case for the States

4

Unlike the NAACP lawyers, who could view the case from one central position, the lawyers representing the states came to the Supreme Court with varying laws and conditions to answer for. This was potentially a disadvantage for the states, especially in light of the fact that the Supreme Court had chosen to hear the cases together in order to deliver a sweeping statement on segregation in public education. By being responsible for only one part of the main case, each of the state attorneys could not be assured that the others would aggressively defend the positions on segregation that his state supported. This concern was well founded, as Kansas, in particular, had no passion for defending segregation—Topeka had already begun to integrate its schools by the time the Court was set to hear oral arguments.

The liberal slant of the Court, the president's stance against segregation, and the growing social and political

The Case for the States

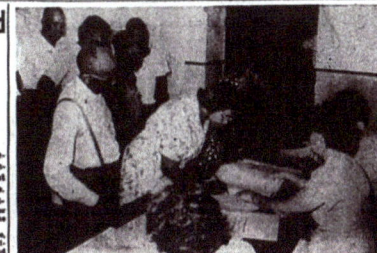

The front page of the Chicago Defender, *an African American newspaper, on July 31, 1948, cheers President Harry Truman's executive order banning segregation in the armed forces. The states defending segregation in the Supreme Court in 1952 knew they could not count on the federal government to support them.*

Brown v. Board of Education

This photograph shows people waiting in line for one of fifty courtroom seats to hear the oral arguments in Brown v. Board of Education *on December 7, 1953.*

trends against racism must have presented additional concerns for the states. Still, the state lawyers knew that the Supreme Court had traditionally been reluctant to order sweeping new changes and that the Court was aware of the difficulties and chaos that could attend the undoing of segregation.

STATES' RIGHTS: A CENTRAL CLAIM

Despite the differences in strategies that the states would take, their arguments were based on the Constitution's Tenth Amendment, which provides, "The powers not delegated to the United States by the Constitution, nor prohibited it to the states,

The Case for the States

are reserved to the states respectively, or to the people." These undefined powers are often referred to as states' rights or police powers. Traditionally, supporters of states' rights subscribe to a narrow reading of the Constitution that holds that if an issue is not specifically mentioned in the Constitution as being the right or power of the president or the Congress, then each state may deal with it as it sees fit.

ARGUMENTS FOR KANSAS

Kansas was represented by its attorney general, Paul E. Wilson, who took great pains to emphasize that the state's law did not endorse segregation, but it allowed its cities the right to decide the issue for themselves. He emphasized that because the lower court in Kansas "found facilities provided for Negro children in the city of Topeka to be substantially equal to those furnished to white children," African American children were not denied equal protection of the laws. He also made the point that the NAACP did not show that any of the children who were directly represented in the case were personally harmed by segregation in, or denied any benefit by, the Topeka schools.

ARGUMENTS FOR SOUTH CAROLINA

In his presentation on behalf of South Carolina, accomplished constitutional scholar John W. Davis noted that the lower court records showed that South Carolina had begun to improve its African American schools. He also questioned the validity of the studies of the social scientists that the NAACP had presented as witnesses in the lower courts.

Brown v. Board of Education

John Davis (left), counsel for South Carolina, and Thurgood Marshall talk before making oral arguments to the Supreme Court. The men were called back by the Court to restate and reargue their positions. This photograph was taken by an Associated Press photographer on December 9, 1952, in Washington, D.C.

Davis made a spirited defense of segregation. He listed seven cases as precedents upholding states' rights to apply racial segregation in local concerns, adding that the issue had been "so often and so pointedly declared by the highest authorities that it should no longer be regarded as open for debate." He insisted that local governments were in a better position than the federal government or the Supreme Court to determine how parents wished their children to be educated.

The following exchange between Davis and Justice Harold Burton demonstrates Davis's narrow reading of the Constitution in favor of states' rights.

The Case for the States

BURTON: What is your answer, Mr. Davis, to the suggestion . . . that at [the time the Fourteenth Amendment was adopted] the conditions and relations between the two races were such that what might have been unconstitutional then would not be unconstitutional now.

DAVIS: My answer to that is that changed conditions may affect policy, but changed conditions cannot broaden the terminology of the Constitution. The thought is an administrative one or a political one, and not a judicial one.

In other words, it is not the Supreme Court's place to make laws, only to determine whether they are constitutional.

ARGUMENTS FOR DELAWARE

State attorney general Albert Young presented the case for Delaware. Young had objected to his cases being combined with the others because he felt that the Supreme Court had not given him enough time (only two weeks) to prepare an adequate brief. This was clearly a disadvantage for the state, which was appealing a lower court ruling that, in effect, ordered the integration of a number of schools.

However, in both his written brief and his oral presentation, Young argued that since the Fourteenth Amendment did not mention public education, the issue was a state concern. He reasoned that the district court in Delaware had committed an error in making its decision because the state was upgrading its

Brown v. Board of Education

black schools to be in compliance with the separate but equal doctrine that was still the law.

ARGUMENTS FOR VIRGINIA

Justin Moore, the legal counsel for the Prince Edward County school board, wrote the brief and made the oral presentation for the state of Virginia. In the brief, he restated the district court finding that Virginia's segregation law was not established without consideration or out of prejudice. Instead, it reflected the traditions of Virginians. Moore argued that segregation was unconstitutional only when it completely denied African Americans their civil rights and noted that this was not the case in Virginia's laws. He, too, argued that the Fourteenth Amendment was not intended to cover local issues such as public schooling. When pressed by the Court to say what he thought would be a constitutional way to end the practice of segregation, he offered that only an amendment to the Constitution could accomplish that.

In both his brief and his oral presentation to the Court, Moore lashed out bitterly against the NAACP and one of its key witnesses, Kenneth Clark. According to Moore, the student strike at Moton High was conducted at the instigation of the NAACP and was not the product of student dissatisfaction. He described Clark as a man of "warped judgement" who had so little knowledge of the South that he was not qualified to speak as a social scientist about its people. Experts on the Supreme Court believe that the justices do not regard such personal attacks favorably.

The Case for the States

The lawyers for Virginia argued that the student plaintiffs from Moton High School, shown in this photograph with some of their parents on the steps of Virginia's capitol, were driven more by NAACP propaganda than by their dissatisfaction with the conditions at the school.

Whatever the inclinations of the justices, the case for the states was made more difficult by the fact that the lower courts had found that three of the four states were shortchanging African American schools and that segregation in the fourth state was in part responsible for feelings of inferiority among African American students. The lawyers had all come to the Court making excuses for their respective states and promising that, on one point or the other, the state had begun or would soon begin to address existing differences. It seemed fair that the NAACP questioned the sincerity of these promises.

{ 39 }

Rearguments and a Decision

5

By all accounts, the Court that heard the case of *Brown v. Board of Education of Topeka* was racked by sharp personal and philosophical divisions, some of which had been exposed to the general public. Although considered to be more liberal than before, the Court had a solid block of conservatives that included Chief Justice Fred Vinson. Vinson was not held in high regard by his colleagues, four of whom considered him an intellectual lightweight. Richard Kluger writes in his book *Simple Justice*, "It was perhaps the most fractured Court in history—testament, on the face of it, to Vinson's failure as Chief Justice."

It is widely believed that upon first deliberating the case, the Supreme Court justices were closely divided. Four justices—Hugo Black, Harold Burton, William Douglas, and Sherman Minton—are seen to have been solidly in favor of

Rearguments and a Decision

The decision for Brown v. Board of Education *was delivered by Chief Justice Earl Warren (seated, front row center, with the 1954 Supreme Court). President Dwight D. Eisenhower appointed Warren, hoping for a moderate conservative. In cases such as* Brown, *Warren showed he was anything but.*

overturning *Plessy*. Stanley Reed was staunchly supportive of segregation. Of the others, Vinson and Tom Clark seemed likely to vote to uphold *Plessy* but order the states to make the separate facilities equal. Felix Frankfurter was likely to vote it down with strong reservations. Robert Jackson was a wild card; it was thought he could go either way.

STALLING FOR TIME

Frankfurter thought that a split vote on such an important decision would be disastrous for the country, especially if the

Brown v. Board of Education

decision had multiple consenting or dissenting opinions. In May 1953, when the Supreme Court term was coming to an end and the justices were still grappling with the case, he devised a plan to give the justices more time to reconcile their differences. The Court placed the case on its schedule for the following term and ordered the lawyers to reargue the case.

The lawyers were asked to provide answers to a list of questions regarding Congress's intention to abolish segregation in public schools in 1868, when it approved the Fourteenth Amendment. There were also questions asking how the Court should go about integrating the schools if it were to decide to end segregation. The Supreme Court also invited the United States attorney general to answer the questions. The reargument was slated for December 7, 1953.

A CHANGE ON THE COURT

Chief Justice Vinson died before the next round of arguments was heard. According to Kluger, Justice Frankfurter responded to the news by saying, "This is the first indication I have ever had that there is a God." Frankfurter was one of the justices who did not think highly of Vinson, and he had given up hope that the chief justice could foster a consensus among the justices in the case.

California governor Earl Warren was appointed to replace Vinson as the chief justice of the Supreme Court. His appointment concerned Thurgood Marshall and the NAACP for two reasons. First, they wondered whether Warren would be sympathetic to the civil rights claims of African Americans considering

Rearguments and a Decision

that, as governor of California, he had overseen the detention of Japanese Americans and the confiscation of their property during World War II. Second, they questioned whether the new Supreme Court justice would be willing to advocate the radical step of overturning the *Plessy* doctrine.

Warren worked diligently to familiarize himself with the issues involved in *Brown v. Board of Education* for the December reargument. Like Frankfurter, he was interested in having the Court speak with one voice on the case. Accordingly, Warren met

R.G. Marshall, a court attendant, helps Supreme Court chief justice Earl Warren put on his robe on October 5, 1953, Warren's first day on the Court. The photograph was taken by an Associated Press photographer and is housed in the Library of Congress.

frequently with his colleagues to assess their positions and quickly developed good working relationships with them. When the day of the reargument finally arrived, he was fully prepared to hear the case.

THE REARGUMENT

During the second round of arguments, the NAACP's lawyers took the position that the broad purpose of congressional approval of the Fourteenth Amendment in 1868 was to abolish

Brown v. Board of Education

segregation in all fields, including education. They argued that it was proper for the current Court to abolish segregation and that not to do so would be akin to saying that African Americans were "inferior to all other human beings." According to Thurgood Marshall, school segregation implied "an inherent determination that the people who were formerly in slavery, regardless of anything else, shall be kept as near that stage as is possible." Imploring the Court to reject that notion, he added, "Now is the time, we submit, that this Court should make it clear that that is not what our Constitution stands for." The NAACP also stated that should the Court decide to end segregation, it should require immediate rather than gradual implementation.

As was expected, the lawyers for the states, led by South Carolina's John Davis, saw the matter differently. Davis asserted that the framers of the Fourteenth Amendment did not intend to outlaw segregation in public schools. To support this point, he noted that even while Congress was drafting the amendment, it had allowed segregated schools in the District of Columbia. Davis warned of the consequences of a desegregation order in Clarendon County, in which there were 2,800 black pupils and 300 white ones:

> Who is going to disturb that situation? If they were to be reassorted or commingled, who knows how that would best be done? If it is done on the mathematical basis, with 30 children as a maximum . . . you would have 27 Negro children and three white ones in one schoolroom. Would that make the children happier? Would they learn any more quickly? . . . Would the terrible psychological disaster being

Rearguments and a Decision

wrought . . . to the colored child be removed if he had three white children sitting somewhere in the same classroom?

These were powerful questions for the justices to ponder.

In its amicus brief and in oral arguments, the federal government, represented by Assistant Attorney General J. Lee Rankin, made it clear that its position was that "segregation in public schools cannot be maintained under the Fourteenth Amendment." The newly elected administration of Dwight Eisenhower supported the integration of public schools but was concerned about southern resistance. Accordingly, it suggested that any desegregation order should allow at least a year for the development of a plan to enforce the order.

THE COURT DECIDES

The Supreme Court justices began deliberating the *Brown* case on December 12, 1953. After hearing the initial thoughts of his associates, Chief Justice Warren realized that a majority of the justices shared his desire to rule against segregation. Determined to achieve a unanimous decision, he worked hard at persuading the opposing justices and developing an opinion that all the justices could support. It took Warren five months to convince the final holdout, Justice Reed, to support his carefully crafted opinion. He had taken great pains to write an opinion in a clear language that the average American would understand. Warren read the Court's ruling to a courtroom full of eager, riveted journalists on May 17, 1954.

Brown v. Board of Education

Thurgood Marshall (center) poses with fellow NAACP lawyers George Hayes (left) and James Nabrit outside the U.S. Supreme Court on May 17, 1954, following the reading of the Court's decision in Brown v. Board of Education. *Hayes and Nabrit had successfully argued a companion case called* Bolling v. Sharpe, *in which the court outlawed racial segregation in public schools in the District of Columbia.*

Warren began with a review of the facts of the case, outlining the claims of the plaintiffs (the parties filing a lawsuit), the findings of the lower courts, the claims made in the two rounds of oral arguments, and the related precedents. He then explained the Court's interpretation of the amendment as it related to public education. He said that the Court could not rely on the language of the amendment or *Plessy v. Ferguson* because public education had come to play a more pivotal role in American life than the framers of the amendment and the justices on the Court in 1896 could have anticipated. The Supreme Court had to consider the current role of public education in American life, which he explained as follows:

> It is required in the performance of our most basic public responsibilities, even service in the armed forces. It is the very foundation of good citizenship. Today it is a principal instrument in awakening the

Rearguments and a Decision

child to cultural values, in preparing him for later professional training, and in helping him adjust normally to his environment.

In answer to what he identified as the central question in the case—"Does segregation of children in public schools solely on the question of race . . . deprive the children of the minority group of equal education opportunities?"—the Court answered, "We believe that it does." The Court also agreed with the NAACP's claims that segregated schools "had a detrimental effect" on black children. In summary, Warren declared:

> We conclude that in the field of public education the doctrine of "separate but equal" has no place. Separate educational facilities are inherently unequal. Therefore, we hold that the plaintiffs and others [in similar situations are] deprived of the equal protection of the laws guaranteed by the Fourteenth Amendment.

After reading the decision, Chief Justice Warren admitted that it would be difficult to implement the Court's decision immediately. In light of this, he asked both sides to submit legal briefs regarding implementation in six months.

REACTIONS TO THE DECISION

Thurgood Marshall and the NAACP were overjoyed by the decision. According to James Tackach in *Brown v. Board of Education*, Marshall would later describe his initial reaction by saying, "I was so happy I was numb." Meanwhile, political leaders in the

Brown v. Board of Education

South reacted with anger. Tackach notes, for example, that Governor Herman Talmadge of Georgia remarked that "the United States Supreme Court had reduced the Constitution to a scrap of paper."

The Court's decision dominated the newspapers on the following day. The opinions of newspaper editors ranged from relief and praise to condemnation and defiance. In an editorial entitled "All God's Chillun," the *New York Times* described the Supreme Court as "the guardian of our national conscience," saying that it had reaffirmed "the undying American faith in the equality of all men and all children before the law." The *Washington Post and Times-Herald* called the ruling "an occasion for pride and gratification."

Mississippi's *Jackson Daily News* issued a blistering attack in its editorial "Bloodstains on White Marble Steps." The article charged, "Human blood may stain Southern soil in many places because of this decision but the dark red stains of that blood will be on the marble steps of the United States Supreme Court Building." It also warned that integrated schools would result in mixed marriages that would lead to the "mongrelization [crossbreeding] of the human race."

Not all the opponents of the ruling were so grim. The University of Mississippi's school paper, the *Mississippian*, offered, "Though the majority of the students do not want to attend school with Negroes, we feel that the students will adapt themselves to it." The *Atlanta Constitution* cautioned, "It is no time to indulge demagogues on either side nor to listen to those who always are ready to incite violence and hate."

Implementation and Impact

6

As Chief Justice Warren had indicated, implementation of the decision would prove difficult. After hearing arguments from all the parties to the case, the Court issued another ruling, known as *Brown v. Board of Education II*, in which it ordered the states to "proceed with all deliberate speed" in integrating their schools. The Court placed the primary responsibility for resolving the problems of desegregation on the school authorities in each school district, but it gave local courts oversight in enforcing the decision.

Predictably, many political leaders in the South presented obstacles to desegregation. The most explosive example took place in Little Rock, Arkansas. In 1957, after a couple of years delaying integration plans, the Little Rock school board announced that nine black students would be

Brown v. Board of Education

The front page of the Topeka State Journal, *the city's afternoon paper, carries the news of the Supreme Court's decision in* Brown v. Board of Education. *It notes that Topeka, Kansas, was already ending racial segregation in schools.*

admitted to Central High School at the start of the 1957–1958 school year. Governor Orval Faubus immediately objected to the plans and ordered the Arkansas National Guard to

{ 50 }

Implementation and Impact

White residents of Little Rock, Arkansas, jeer Elizabeth Eckford, one of the Little Rock Nine, as she walks toward Central High School on September 6, 1957. Armed soldiers watch the action from the sidelines.

surround the school on opening day to prevent the black students from entering the compound. President Eisenhower was able to convince Faubus to withdraw the guardsmen the following day. But the tone had already been set. For several days, unruly mobs surrounded and taunted the Little Rock Nine, as the group of students came to be called, on their way to school. Eventually, President Eisenhower dispatched one thousand soldiers and ten thousand guardsmen to protect the students from the mob. They were there for more than two months.

But the school board and Governor Faubus remained undaunted in their efforts to undermine the decision. The

{ 51 }

Brown v. Board of Education

TIMELINE

1619 Slavery begins in the United States when African slaves are brought to Jamestown, Virginia, and sold to planters.

1861–1865 The American Civil War is fought.

1863 President Abraham Lincoln issues the Emancipation Proclamation.

1865 The Thirteenth Amendment abolishes slavery; Reconstruction begins; Mississippi passes the first black code limiting the rights of African Americans; the Ku Klux Klan is founded.

1866 Congress passes civil rights legislation.

1868 The Fourteenth Amendment grants citizenship and certain civil rights to African Americans.

1870 The Fifteenth Amendment gives African American males the right to vote.

1877 Reconstruction ends.

1896 The U.S. Supreme Court establishes the "separate but equal" principle in the *Plessy v. Ferguson* decision.

1909 The NAACP is founded.

1939 The NAACP establishes its legal defense fund.

1950 In *Sweatt v. Painter* and *McLaurin v. Oklahoma State Regents*, the Supreme Court establishes that the separate but equal standard is unattainable in state-sponsored higher education.

1954 Separate but equal is ruled to be unconstitutional in the *Brown v. Board of Education* Supreme Court decision.

1955 *Brown v. Board of Education II* outlines a plan for implementing desegregation.

1957 President Eisenhower sends soldiers and National Guardsmen to Little Rock, Arkansas, to escort nine black students to Central High School.

Implementation and Impact

Buddy Trammell, Max Stiles, and Tommy Sanders (left to right), *three white students at Clinton High School in Clinton, Tennessee, hold signs protesting the integration of their school on August 27, 1956. Protests like these were common when the U.S. government tried to implement the 1954 Supreme Court decision throughout the South.*

following year, they closed Central High and arranged for the white students to attend private schools. The Little Rock Nine were forced to return to their old Jim Crow schools. Finally, in June 1959, a U.S. district court ordered the reopening of Central High on a non-segregated basis. More than a decade following the Supreme Court decisions, the federal government and the courts continued to struggle to get many southern school districts to comply.

Brown v. Board of Education

The Rev. Martin Luther King delivers his "I Have a Dream" speech to a large civil rights gathering during the March on Washington on August 28, 1963. African Americans were emboldened by the NAACP's victory in Brown v. Board of Education to step up their demands for civil rights.

IMPACT

Ironically, the *Brown v. Board of Education* decision is widely seen as having a greater impact on other areas of American life than it did on public education. The decision served as a rallying call for African Americans, who used it to demand other rights. It spurred the civil rights movement of the 1950s and 1960s, which resulted in the dismantling of racial segregation in other walks of life. The passage of the Civil Rights Act of 1964, which bans discrimination in voting, employment, and public accommodations, was a direct outgrowth of this newfound black activism. And the African American civil rights movement has been widely regarded for having paved the way for other civil rights movements, such as women's rights and gay rights.

Glossary

abolitionist   Person who advocated an end to slavery.

amicus curiae   A person or entity who is not a party to a lawsuit but who presents a point of view for the court to consider.

appeal   To ask for a review of the results of a lower case trial in a higher court.

brief   Written legal argument outlining the laws and facts presented by a party to a lawsuit.

civil disobedience   Refusal to obey civil laws by nonviolent means in an effort to change legislation.

civil rights   The fundamental rights belonging to individuals by nature of citizenship or legal residency.

class-action lawsuit   A lawsuit that is pursued on behalf of a large group of people who claim to have been wronged by a defendant in a similar way.

demagogue   A leader who obtains power by preying on the emotions and prejudices of the people.

dissenting opinion   The opinion of a judge or judges who disagree with the opinion of the majority of the court.

freedman   A person freed from slavery.

Brown v. Board of Education

ideal   An honorable principle or goal.

lynching   To execute (especially by hanging) without due process of the law, as by a mob.

opinion   The written explanation of the decision of a judge or group of judges in a trial.

segregate   To separate (a race or a class) from a main group.

states' rights   The undefined powers granted to the states by the Tenth Amendment of the U.S. Constitution.

white supremacy   A belief that white people are superior and should dominate society.

For More Information

National Association for the Advancement of Colored People (NAACP)

4805 Mt. Hope Drive

Baltimore, MD 21215

(877) NAACP-98 (622-2798)

Web site: http://www.naacp.org

U.S. Supreme Court

One First Street NE

Washington, DC 20543

(888) 293-6498

(202) 512-1530

Web site: http://www.supremecourtus.gov

Web Sites

Due to the changing nature of Internet links, the Rosen Publishing Group, Inc., has developed an online list of Web sites related to the subject of this book. This site is updated regularly. Please use this link to access the list:

http://www.rosenlinks.com/scctps/brbe

For Further Reading

Baker, Ray S. *Following the Color Line: American Citizenship in the Progressive Era*. New York: Harper & Row, 1964.

Fireside, Harvey. *Brown v. Board of Education: Equal Schooling for All*. Berkeley Heights, NJ: Enslow Publishers, Inc., 1994.

Fireside, Harvey. *Plessy v. Ferguson*. Berkeley Heights, NJ: Enslow Publishers, Inc., 1997.

Foner, Eric. *A Short History of Reconstruction*. New York: Harper & Row, 1990.

Tackach, James. *Brown v. Board of Education* (Famous Trials). San Diego: Lucent Books, 1998.

Bibliography

Du Bois, W. E. B. *The Souls of Black Folk*. New York: Penguin USA, 1996.

Edwards, George C., III, Martin P. Wattenberg, and Robert L. Lineberry. *Government in America: People, Politics, and Policy*. New York: HarperCollins, 1997.

Fireside, Harvey. *Brown v. Board of Education: Equal Schooling for All*. Berkeley Heights, NJ: Enslow Publishers, Inc., 1994.

Fireside, Harvey. *Plessy v. Ferguson*. Berkeley Heights, NJ: Enslow Publishers, Inc., 1997.

Kluger, Richard. *Simple Justice*. New York: Vintage Books, 1975.

Lofgren, Charles A. *The Plessy Case: A Legal-Historical Interpretation*. New York: Oxford University Press, 1987.

Martin, Waldo E., Jr. *Brown v. Board of Education: A Brief History with Documents*. Boston: Bedford/St. Martin's, 1998.

Mullane, Deirdre, ed. *Crossing the Danger Water: Three Hundred Years of African-American Writing*. New York: Anchor Books, 1993.

Orfield, Gary, Susan E. Eaton, and the Harvard Project on School Desegregation. *Dismantling Segregation: The Quiet Reversal of Brown v. Board of Education*. New York: The New Press, 1996.

Patterson, James. *Brown v. Board of Education: A Civil Rights Milestone and Its Troubled Legacy*. New York: Oxford University Presss, 2001.

Tackach, James. *Brown v. Board of Education* (Famous Trials). San Diego, CA: Lucent Books, 1998.

Thomas, Brook, ed. *Plessy v. Ferguson: A Brief History with Documents*. Boston: Bedford/St. Martin's, 1997.

Tuttle, Kate. "Brown v. Board of Education." Africana.com. Retrieved November 2002 (http://www.africana.com/Articles/tt_100.htm).

Wilson, Paul E. *A Time to Lose: Representing Kansas in Brown v. Board of Education*. Lawrence, KS: University of Kansas, 1995.

Primary Source Image List

Cover: Photograph of Linda Brown in her classroom at the Monroe School. Taken in Topeka, Kansas, in March 1953 by Carl Iwasaki.

Page 6: Cartoon titled "And Remember, Nothing Can Be Accomplished by Taking to the Streets." Illustrated by Herbert Block. Published in the *Washington Post* on September 6, 1963. Housed in the Library of Congress.

Page 9: Photograph of the Rex Theatre in Leland, Mississippi. Taken by Marion Post Wolcott in November 1939.

Page 10: Photograph of a banner hanging from the NAACP headquarters in New York City. Taken in 1936. Housed in the Library of Congress.

Page 12: Photograph of a segregated, one-roomed, black school in Georgia. Taken in 1941.

Page 15: Photograph of a woman recruiting members to the NAACP.

Page 16: Cover of the first issue of *The Crisis*, from November 1910. Published in New York City.

Page 17: Photograph of Thurgood Marshall.

Page 18: Flier for the March on Washington. Created in 1941. From the A. Philip Randolph Institute, Manuscript Division.

Page 21: Photograph of Linda Brown and Terry Lynn Brown walking along railroad tracks. Taken by Carol Iwasaki in 1954 in Topeka, Kansas.

Page 25: Photograph of Tuskegee Airmen. Taken in 1945 by Toni Frissell. Housed in the Library of Congress, Prints and Photographs Division.

Page 27: Photograph of George McLaurin sitting in a segregated anteroom in a graduate class. Taken at the University of Oklahoma in 1948. Housed in the Library of Congress.

Page 29: (Top) Photograph of white elementary school in South Boston, Virginia. (Bottom) Photograph of African American elementary school in South Boston, Virginia. Both housed in the Library of Congress.

Page 33: Front page of the *Chicago Defender*. Extra edition printed on July 31, 1948. Archived in the Library of Congress.

Page 34: Photograph of spectators outside the *Brown v. Board of Education* case. Taken on December 7, 1953, at the Supreme Court in Washington, D.C. From the Library of Congress, Prints and Photographs Division, New York World-Telegram and the Sun Newspaper Photograph Collection.

Primary Source Image List

Page 36: Photograph of John W. Davis and Thurgood Marshall. Taken by an Associated Press photographer in Washington, D.C., on December 9, 1952.

Page 39: Photograph of plaintiffs from *Davis v. County School Board of Prince Edward County*. Taken in Richmond, Virginia. Housed in the Schomburg Center for Research in Black Culture.

Page 41: Photograph of the 1954 Supreme Court. Taken by Fabian Bachrach. From the Collection of the Supreme Court of the United States.

Page 43: Photograph of R. G. Marshall and Earl Warren. Taken by an Associated Press photographer in Washington, D.C., in 1953. Housed in the Library of Congress.

Page 46: Photograph of George Hayes, Thurgood Marshall, and James Nabrit outside the U.S. Supreme Court. Taken by an Associated Press photographer in Washington, D.C., on May 17, 1954.

Page 50: Front page of the *Topeka State Journal*, May 17, 1954. Housed in the Kansas State Historical Society.

Page 51: Photograph of Elizabeth Eckford walking to Central High School. Taken in Little Rock, Arkansas, on September 6, 1957.

Page 53: Photograph of Buddy Trammell, Max Stiles, and Tommy Sanders in Clinton, Tennessee. Taken by an Associated Press photographer on August 27, 1956.

Page 54: Photograph of Martin Luther King Jr. speaking at the March on Washington. Taken in Washington, D.C., on August 28, 1963, by Bob Henriques.

Index

A

African Americans, 4, 6, 10–12, 13, 25–26
    civil rights of, 4, 7, 13, 15, 38, 42, 54
    inferior facilities for, 10, 11, 15
    limited freedoms of, 6, 8, 9–10
    and right to vote, 5, 10
    as teachers, 11, 15
Amendment, Fifteenth, 6, 14
Amendment, Fourteenth, 6, 14, 28, 37, 38, 42, 43, 44, 45, 46, 47
Amendment, Tenth, 34
Amendment, Thirteenth, 6, 14

B

Black, Hugo, 40
Briggs v. Elliott, 19–20, 23, 28, 31, 35–37
Brown v. Board of Education of Topeka, Kansas, 7, 19, 20–21, 23, 28, 40, 46
    briefs for, 24, 28, 30, 31, 37, 45, 47
    lawyers for the NAACP in, 19, 20, 21, 22, 23, 24–31, 32, 35, 43, 44
    lawyers for the states in, 32, 34, 35–38, 43, 44
    oral arguments for, 24, 28, 35, 45
    rearguments for, 42, 43–45
    Supreme Court decision, 45–47, 48, 49, 53, 54
    Supreme Court hearings, 23, 27–31, 32–39
Brown v. Board of Education II, 49
Burton, Harold, 36–37, 40

C

Carter, Robert, 21, 24, 28
Civil Rights Act, 54
Clark, Kenneth, 38
Clark, Tom, 41
Crisis, The, 14

D

Davis, John W., 35–37, 44
Davis v. County School Board of Prince Edward County, Virginia, 19, 22–23, 28, 31, 38–39
Delaware cases, 19, 21–22, 23, 28, 31, 37–38
Douglas, William, 40
Du Bois, W. E. B., 11–12, 14

E

Eisenhower, Dwight, 45, 51

F

Faubus, Orval, 50–53
Frankfurter, Felix, 41–42, 43

G

Greenberg, Jack, 21, 22, 24, 28

Index

H
Houston, Charles, 15, 17

J
Jackson, Robert, 41
Jim Crow laws, 8, 10, 11, 12, 13, 31, 53

L
Little Rock Nine, 49–53

M
Marshall, Thurgood, 15, 18, 19, 20, 21, 24, 25, 28, 30, 42, 44, 47
McLaurin v. Oklahoma State Regents for Higher Education, 26, 30
Minton, Sherman, 40
Moore, Justin, 38
Myrdal, Gunnar, 26

N
National Association for the Advancement of Colored People (NAACP), 13, 14–15, 17, 18, 19, 21, 22, 24, 25, 26, 27, 28, 30, 31, 32, 38, 39, 42, 43, 44, 47

P
Plessy v. Ferguson, 6, 8, 9, 17, 18–19, 24, 26, 27, 30, 31, 40, 43, 46

R
Rankin, J. Lee, 45
Redding, Louis, 22
Reed, Stanley, 41, 45
Robinson, Spottswood, 22, 24, 28

S
schools, public, 7, 11, 15, 24, 28, 32, 37, 38, 42, 44, 45, 46, 47, 54
for African Americans, 11, 13, 15, 17–18, 19, 20, 21, 22, 23, 31, 35, 38, 39
differences in segregated, 11, 17, 19, 22, 26, 30
graduate, 17, 26–27, 30
integration of, 28, 31, 32, 37, 42, 45, 49–53
psychological impact of segregated, 20, 21, 22, 30, 35, 39, 44–45, 47
Seitz, Collins, 22
"separate but equal," 6, 17, 22, 26, 30, 31, 38, 41, 47
states' rights, 34–35, 36
Sweatt v. Painter, 26, 30

T
Talmadge, Herman, 48
Truman, Harry, 31

U
U.S. Congress, 8, 14, 15, 35, 42, 44
U.S. Constitution, 6, 9, 10, 26, 34, 35, 36, 37, 38, 44, 48
U.S. Supreme Court, 4–6, 7, 8, 20, 22, 23, 24, 26, 27, 28, 30, 31, 32, 34, 36, 37, 38, 39, 40, 42, 44, 47, 48, 49, 53
justices, 26, 30, 36–37, 38, 39, 40–43, 45

V
Vinson, Fred, 40, 41, 42

W
Warren, Earl, 42–43, 45–47, 49
Wilson, Paul E., 35
World War II, 25, 43

Y
Young, Albert, 37–38

Brown v. Board of Education

About the Author

Wayne Anderson is a freelance writer and editor who lives in New York City. A native of Jamaica, he is a former music editor for the *New York Carib News*, the largest Caribbean American newsweekly in the United States, and the author of four books for young adults. A self-described postmodernist, he maintains an intense interest in the stories of "the others" in society. He is currently working on a collection of poems.

Photo Credits

Eagle on back cover and throughout interior © Eyewire; red curtain throughout interior © Arthur S. Aubry/PhotoDisc; wood grain on cover and back cover and throughout interior © M. Angelo/Corbis; Cover, p. 21 © Carl Iwasaki/TimePix; pp. 6, 25, 27, 29, 34, 43 Library of Congress, Prints and Photographs Division; p. 9 © Hulton/Archive/Getty Images; pp. 10, 15 © Corbis; pp. 12, 16, 51 © Bettmann/Corbis; p. 17 National Archive and Records Administration; p. 18 Library of Congress, Manuscript Division; p. 33 Library of Congress, Serial and Government Publications Division; pp. 36, 46, 53 © AP/Wide World Photos; p. 39 Prints and Photographs Division, Schomburg Center for Research in Black Culture, The New York Public Library; p. 41 Fabian Bachrach/Collection of the Supreme Court of the United States; p. 50 The Kansas State Historical Society, Topeka, Kansas; p. 54 © Bob Henriques/Magnum Photos.

Designer: Evelyn Horovicz; Editor: Christine Poolos; Photo Researcher: Amy Feinberg.

www.ingramcontent.com/pod-product-compliance
Lightning Source LLC
Chambersburg PA
CBHW041115070526
44584CB00002B/179